So precious ... like a teacup
God's love ... the best kind of tea!

Presented to: _____

From: _____

Date: _____

The Precious Teacup

by Heather Johnson
Illustrations- by Ken Save

AuthorHouse™
1663 Liberty Drive
Bloomington, IN 47403
www.authorhouse.com
Phone: 1-800-839-8640

Thank you to those who helped to make this book a reality: my parents, my family and friends, my pastors and church family at Christian Life Assembly, my husband Ben and our four precious daughters. Also a special thank you to some newfound friends - I couldn't have done this without you all. to the illustrator, Ken Save, thank you for taking the pictures right out of my heart and mind and putting them to paper so beautifully! to Andrew Jaster, thanks for a great job of desktop publishing and web design. and to Ed Strauss, thanks! behind every author is a good editor. And most of all - to my Lord and Savior, Jesus, who is the giver and the releaser of dreams!

www.thepreciousteacup.com

First published by AuthorHouse 3/4/2011

ISBN: 978-1-4567-3144-1 (sc)

Library of Congress Control Number: 2011903773

Printed in the United States of America

This book is printed on acid-free paper.

authorHOUSE®

Dedicated to Chelsea, Dania, Aislyn and Bretta.

"Like clay in the hand of the potter, so are you in my hand." - Jeremiah 18:6 (NIV)

A teacup is so precious,
It's made to hold some tea.

In many ways
I'm like it;
Now, would
you like to see?

The Potter makes the teacup
He shapes it out of clay.

God made me very special
He made me his own way.

Its color is
so pretty,
The teacup
has design;

There is no one
just like me.
God's plan
is so divine.

But dust and
dirt can settle
And germs
at times get in;

God's Word says
he can clean me,
And take
away my sin.

So with a final washing
The teacup now is new.

When I ask for forgiveness
God can clean me, too!

The teacup has been bought now,
So I can have some tea;

I give my life to Jesus:
He paid the price for me!

Now beautiful
and ready,
It's time to
fill this cup.

The Potter
is my Master,
With love
he fills me up!

Each teacup holds the finest-
Just try it and you'll see.

This love that comes from Jesus
Is absolutely free!

This tea is meant for sharing;
At parties and with friends.

God's love is overflowing,
It never, ever ends.

I love my little teacup
My teacup helps me see,

That to Jesus,
I am precious–
His love is
full in me!

Dear Jesus,

Thank you for making me so precious. Please clean me inside and take away my sin. Thank you for giving your life for me, so I can live forever with you. I believe you are alive today and I invite you to come into my heart and to fill me with your love.

I love you Jesus!
Amen.

"…God has poured out his love into our hearts…"

- Romans 5:5

"I praise you because I am fearfully and wonderfully made; your works are wonderful, I know that full well."

- Psalm 139:14

Author Bio: Heather Johnson, is the author and founder of the Precious Teacup Series. Her passion is to share an urgent message of grace that would transform little girls lives around our globe- instilling hope, value, and salvation. Together with her husband, Ben, she shares a calling. They minister to this next generation through creative outreach initiatives and leadership development. The Johnsons reside in Langley, BC Canada, with their four daughters.

Artist Bio: Ken Save and his wife, Vickie, live in Pitt Meadows, British Columbia, where Ken earns his living as an illustrator. Ken has illustrated over 100 books for Zondervan (he helped illustrate The Amazing Treasure Bible), Focus on the Family, Tyndale, Barbour and other Christian publishers. He has drawn Star Trek comics for D.C. Comics and in recent years has illustrated children's books such as *Children, Can You Hear Me?* and *The Precious Teacup*.

CPSIA information can be obtained at www.ICGtesting.com
Printed in the USA
LVIW01n2220150816
500527LV00006B/11